Hispanic Heritage

Hispanic Heritage

Title List

Central American Immigrants to the United States: Refugees from Unrest

Cuban Americans: Exiles from an Island Home

First Encounters Between Spain and the Americas: Two Worlds Meet

Latino Americans and Immigration Laws: Crossing the Border

Latino Americans in Sports, Film, Music, and Government: Trailblazers

Latino Arts and Their Influence on the United States: Songs, Dreams, and Dances

Latino Cuisine and Its Influence on American Foods: The Taste of Celebration

Latino Economics in the United States: Job Diversity

Latino Folklore and Culture: Stories of Family, Traditions of Pride

Latino Migrant Workers: America's Harvesters

Latinos Today: Facts and Figures

The Latino Religious Experience: People of Faith and Vision

Mexican Americans' Role in the United States: A History of Pride, A Future of Hope

Puerto Ricans' History and Promise: Americans Who Cannot Vote

South America's Immigrants to the United States: The Flight from Turmoil

The Story of Latino Civil Rights: Fighting for Justice

South America's Immigrants to the United States

The Flight from Turmoil

by Kenneth and Marsha McIntosh

Mason Crest Publishers
Philadelphia

Mason Crest Publishers Inc.

370 Reed Road

Broomall, Pennsylvania 19008

(866) MCP-BOOK (toll free)

First printing

1 2 3 4 5 6 7 8 9 10

Library of Congress Cataloging-in-Publication Data

McIntosh, Kenneth, 1959–
  South American immigrants to the United States : flight from turmoil / by Kenneth and Marsha McIntosh.
     p. cm. — (Hispanic heritage)
  Includes bibliographical references and index.
  ISBN 1-59084-930-2 ISBN 1-59084-924-8 (series)
  1. South American Americans— Social conditions—Juvenile literature. I. McIntosh, Marsha. II. Title. III. Hispanic heritage (Philadelphia, Pa.)
  E184.S75M426 2005
  973'.0468—dc22

                                    2004024624

Produced by Harding House Publishing Service, Inc., Vestal, NY.

Interior design by Dianne Hodack and MK Bassett-Harvey.

Cover design by Dianne Hodack.

Printed in the Hashemite Kingdom of Jordan.

Contents

by José E. Limón, Ph.D.

ven before there was a United States, Hispanics were present in what would become this country. Beginning in the sixteenth century, Spanish explorers traversed North America, and their explorations encouraged settlement as early as the sixteenth century in what is now northern New Mexico and Florida, and as late as the mid-eighteenth century in what is now southern Texas and California.

Later, in the nineteenth century, following Spain's gradual withdrawal from the New World, Mexico in particular established its own distinctive presence in what is now the southwestern part of the United States, a presence reinforced in the first half of the twentieth century by substantial immigration from that country. At the close of the nineteenth century, the U.S. war with Spain brought Cuba and Puerto Rico into an interactive relationship with the United States, the latter in a special political and economic affiliation with the United States even as American power influenced the course of almost every other Latin American country.

The books in this series remind us of these historical origins, even as each explores the present reality of different Hispanic groups. Some of these books explore the contemporary social origins—what social scientists call the "push" factors—behind the accelerating Hispanic immigration to America: political instability, economic underdevelopment and crisis, environmental degradation, impoverished or wholly absent educational systems, and other circumstances contribute to many Latin Americans deciding they will be better off in the United States.

And, for the most part, they will be. The vast majority come to work and work very hard, in order to earn better wages than they would back home. They fill significant labor needs in the U.S. economy and contribute to the economy through lower consumer prices and sales taxes.

When they leave their home countries, many immigrants may initially fear that they are leaving behind vital and important aspects of their home cultures: the Spanish language, kinship ties, food, music, folklore, and the arts. But as these books also make clear, culture is a fluid thing, and these native cultures are not only brought to America, they are also replenished in the United States in fascinating and novel ways. These books further suggest to us that Hispanic groups enhance American culture as a whole.

Our country—especially the young, future leaders who will read these books—can only benefit by the fair and full knowledge these authors provide about the socio-historical origins and contemporary cultural manifestations of America's Hispanic heritage.

There were just two words written on the letter:

"*Revolucionario, beware!*"

Lucas Cardona was working as a *community advocate* in the Antioquia region of Colombia when he found the note tucked under his front door. He had been falsely accused of siding with the *guerrilla* army, one side in the bloody Colombian civil war. (Kristen Lombardi told Cardona's story in an article for the *Boston Phoenix* newspaper.)

community advocate: someone who speaks on behalf of their community to those in authority.

guerrilla: a person who engages in irregular warfare, especially as a member of an independent unit carrying out harassment and sabotage campaigns.

Artwork

Gourd art illustrates the pattern of everyday South American life.

amnesty: a general pardon by the government to those who have committed illegal acts.

Months later, Lucas and his friend Luis were relaxing in a popular downtown nightclub. The party atmosphere was shattered suddenly by the sounds of gunfire. Lucas felt a sharp pain. Glancing down at his legs, he saw blood. A bullet had ripped through both his right thigh and left leg.

Terrified, the assassins would return and finish him off, he knew then that he would have to leave Colombia quickly. Cardona paid $2,000 to obtain a fake visa, which would enable him to travel to the United States. Two weeks later, he arrived in Boston, Massachusetts.

Lucas's friend Luis remained in Colombia. Six months after Lucas traveled to the United States, Luis was killed. Assassins gunned him down at point-blank range.

Meanwhile, in the United States, Cardona fared much better. Kristen Lombardi describes his new life in her article:

> In the seven years since his desperate flight, Cardona . . . has fashioned a rather normal life for himself: he works as an artist in and around Boston; he met and settled down with his wife in this area; they have a three-year-old son, Mitchell. To this day, however, Cardona is haunted by fear—not of being killed, but of being sent back to a place where he will be.

Cardona is typical of Colombian immigrants living in the United States. For the most part, they are young, educated men and women who can afford to escape from the violence in their homeland. This violence is a large-scale tragedy. Every month, two hundred people are kidnapped. Each year, 3,000 are murdered. More than a million have been removed from their homes by political violence.

Considering these dire statistics, you might think Lucas Cardona would be granted the privilege of political *amnesty*, including the right to live legally in the United States, as a place

War on Drugs

The term "War on Drugs" was first used by President Richard Nixon in 1972 to describe government actions to eliminate the use of illegal recreational drugs, including marijuana, heroin, and cocaine. President Ronald Reagan added the position of "drug czar" to the Cabinet. First Lady Nancy Reagan's "Just Say No" campaign was a very visible part of the War on Drugs.

There are three primary means of attack in the War on Drugs:

- specialized law-enforcement agencies, officers, and techniques
- educational campaigns focusing on the dangers of drug use
- loosened enforcement and evidence-gathering procedures and requirement

There is no evidence that such campaigns actually curtail drug use. Additionally, the loosened law-enforcement requirements cause concern among many about potential civil liberties violations.

The United States is not the only country with a War on Drugs. Most countries have some kind of antidrug program in place.

of shelter from the threat of death in his own country. For centuries, the United States has provided refuge to people fleeing from oppression and hardship around the world. But Cardona and other Colombian refugees like him are caught on the horns of U.S. policy toward Colombia—and Lucas's application was denied. "It's very hard for Colombians to be defined as political refugees in the United States," he says.

The United States pays the Colombian government vast amounts of money to fight against revolutionary guerrillas who support themselves by trafficking drugs. Colombia is considered a "democratic ally" of the United States, which means if the American government allowed Colombian immigrants like Cardona to receive amnesty as political refugees, it would appear to be criticizing the Colombian government. That admission might interfere with America's War on Drugs. As a result, persons like Lucas, who face death threats in Colombia, are denied the right to legal refuge in the United States.

Cardona wishes that Congress would help the Colombians who are in this country. He says that Colombian immigrants have worked hard, raised families, paid taxes, and contributed to North American society. "In Colombia," he says, "the people have no freedom, no opportunity, no chance to thrive." He adds, "Colombians can be good citizens in this country—if we are given the chance."

en and women leave their homes in South America and begin new lives in the United States for a variety of

Children's lives are especially affected by the poverty in South America.

emigration: the act of leaving one's native country to live in another country.

An Example of Ethnic Diversity

In our increasingly diverse world, there are greater numbers of people—in every nation—whose background cannot be limited to one culture or race. For example, pop music sensation Shakira owes her beautiful features—and her stirring musical compositions—to a combination of her mother's Colombian and her father's Lebanese backgrounds.

reasons, and in a variety of circumstances. Some, like Lucas Cardona, come seeking safety and freedom. More come looking for economic opportunities.

In the past decades, South America's large cities have experienced tremendous numbers of poor people moving in from the countryside. Many South American cities today are crowded with poor people who came seeking jobs—and have found only more dire poverty. This migration of rural poor within South America has created a new wave of *emigration*—a movement out of South America to the north. Middle-class South Americans leave the crowded cities and struggling economies of their homelands seeking greater possibilities in *los Estados Unidos* (the United States).

South American immigrants come from a variety of cultural and racial backgrounds. Some are what most Anglo-Americans expect: dark-skinned, dark-haired Spanish-speakers. Others, however, are fair-skinned, blue-eyed people of recent European ancestry. Some are pure-blooded Inca Indians, who speak their own ancient Quechua dialect. People migrating from Brazil, which is South America's largest nation, speak Portuguese rather than Spanish. Immigrants coming from the South American nation of Guyana are either of African or East Indian descent and speak English, Hindi, or Urdu languages.

A Growing Minority

he immigration of South Americans to the United States—along with their more numerous neighbors from

A Few Statistics

he numbers of immigrants to the United States from South America are relatively small compared to the numbers of people coming from other continents. The most recent data comes from the 2000 Census, and counts immigrants who have come to the United States since 1970. Of the top twenty nations of origin for immigrants to the United States, only three are South American:

- 435,000 immigrants are reported from Colombia
- 328,000 from Peru
- 281,000 from Ecuador

These nations rank tenth, seventeenth, and twentieth among all the nations from which people migrate to the United States. The numbers of South American immigrants are pretty small compared to the almost eight million who came from Mexico, or one and a half million from China.

From all South American countries combined there were 1,876,000 immigrants since 1970 documented by the 2000 Census. That's 100,000 less than the number reported from the smaller region of Central America. However, undocumented immigrants tend to avoid being counted in official government censuses, so the number of South American immigrants—especially Colombians—is probably somewhat greater than the Census Bureau records.

In some neighborhoods in Miami, you hear only Spanish spoken.

Central America and Mexico—is transforming the face of the United States. At the beginning of the twenty-first century, Latinos have become the dominant minority group in the United States. Hispanics now comprise nearly 13 percent of the U.S. population. The Latino population in the United States nearly doubled between 1990 and 2004—from 22.4 million to almost 40 million.

In his book *Latino History and Culture*, D. H. Figueredo writes:

It is possible to live in Miami without uttering a word of English. You can shop at a supermarket owned by Cubans, visit an Uruguayan doctor, buy medicine from a pharmacy owned by a Chilean, and socialize at restaurants with folks from the Dominican Republic.

You can vote for a Spanish-speaking official and listen to the news in Spanish. You can go for days without hearing English spoken.

And Miami is not the only city in the United States where the Latino population is booming.

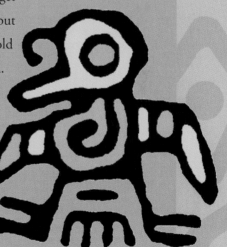

Miami is home to many Latinos.

lexander Agoado's grandmother knew by the age of fourteen that she wanted to come to the United States where there were far more opportunities available to women. In her native country of Colombia, women were expected to get married and have children but not pursue an education—but she had attended an American school run by women who told her she could do most anything she wanted, if she only tried.

When she was nineteen, she visited a cousin in New York City, and she became even more convinced that she wanted to live in the United States. She returned to Colombia and went to work for an airline so she could earn money as well as a free ticket to travel to the United States again. Finally, in 1965 when she was twenty-one, Alexander's grandmother asked her cousin in New York to sponsor her so she could enter the United States permanently.

At first she shared a rented room with her cousin and her older brother who had already immigrated to the United States. She got a job as a clerk at a dentistry school and in two and a half years worked her way up to secretary. She married and had two children, and at the same time she pursued a college education, attending night school for seven years. Finally, she graduated with honors, and then went on to earn her Ph.D. in 1991.

Diana Olivos from Queens, New York, heard a similar story about her father José's emigration from Peru:

When I came to the United States of America, I was thirteen. I arrived on September 5, 1965, by airplane. I was looking forward to coming but sad to leave Peru, my country. I was able to bring all my personal belongings. My family (my mother and two older brothers) were here to meet me when I arrived at JFK. I went to live in Jackson Heights, Queens, with my mother and my older brothers.

The following week, I went to school about five blocks away from where I lived. There was an elementary school one block from my house where I met a boy named Kent the very first day I arrived. It turned out that Kent and I were in the same school and same class. Kent helped me adapt to the English language. We became friends and still are. When we finished intermediate school we went to high school and college together. We went to Newtown High School and City College [of the City University of New York].

Hispanic neighborhood in New York City

I became a citizen in 1978. I never moved back to Peru, but one of my brothers did over the years. While I was here I went to a church called the Community Methodist Church of Jackson Heights. I still go there with my family. I'm glad I came here because of the family I now have. I'm glad my children were born here and are getting a good education that will help them with the rest of their lives. Because I came here as a child I don't really miss Peru. I have family and I call them and e-mail them to keep in touch. I visit them once in a while. Coming to America was a great choice my mother made.

Where Do They Live?

he 2000 Census reports the numbers of persons living in the United States from South American nations of origin and the cities they live in. There are South American immigrants living in practically every city in the country, but these were the top five:

New York, New York	383,000
Miami, Florida	224,000
Los Angeles & Long Beach, California	133,000
Washington, D.C.	94,000
Fort Lauderdale, Florida	93,000

Ashley Prashad's grandfather emigrated from Guyana to the United States in 1972 because he was looking for better economic and educational opportunities. He knew the United States was a prosperous and industrialized nation. At first, however, living in America was a challenge because he came to a different environment with no family or friends; he had to seek employment to support himself and his family back home in South America, a difficult task since he was an undocumented immigrant. Coming from a tropical country as he did, the Northeast's harsh winters were especially hard for him. He

Many South American immigrants build successful lives in the United States.

needed a place to live and warmer clothing. Fortunately he found a good job that sponsored him, allowing him to live here legally, and he was eventually able to send for his family so that they could come to America as legal immigrants.

Despite the hardships and challenges, Ashley's grandfather succeeded in making a productive life for himself and his family. His children were able to receive a quality education; he was able to purchase a house in a few years and to provide for his family's needs. Immigrating to the United States proved to be a good decision for her grandfather. Today, he is proud to be an American.

South America

ꫛabla ꫛspañol

emigrar (ae-me-grahr): to emigrate, leave one's country

imigrar (ee-me-grahr): to immigrate, settle in a new country

imingrante (ee-meen-gron-tay): immigrant, a person settling in another country

Don't Know Much About Geography?

o understand immigrants from South America, a basic understanding of the geography of this continent is helpful. South America is the fourth largest continent on the globe, covering an area of 6,878,000 square miles (17,813,900 sq. km.). Along the Pacific (West) Coast, the Andes Mountains extend along most of the length of the continent. The Andes are the world's longest mountain chain, stretching more than 5,000 miles (12,949.9 kilometers), twice the length of the United States if you measured from east to west coasts. On the Atlantic side of South America, the Amazon River is the largest body of fresh water in the world, providing moisture to the world's largest tropical rain forests.

Brazil is the largest nation in South America, with more than three million square miles (7,769,960 sq. km.). Brazil's 174 million citizens speak Portuguese as their national language. The most famous Brazilian cities are Rio de Janeiro and São Paulo, but the capital of the country is Brasilia.

The Andes Mountain region of South America consists of the countries of Bolivia, Colombia, Ecuador, Peru, and Venezuela. This region produces many export crops such as coffee, cotton, cocoa beans, potatoes, and sugar. The region is also a major exporter of illegal crops—marijuana and cocaine. Colombia is the most populous nation in the Andes, with more than 40 million inhabitants; then comes Peru with 27 million, followed by Venezuela with 23 million. Along the north Atlantic coast of South America are the smaller nations of Guyana, Surinam, and French Guyana.

The southern part of South America is home to the nations of Argentina, with 37 million inhabitants; Chile, with 15 million; Paraguay, with almost six million; and Uruguay, with three million. North Americans often assume that all the nations south of the United States enjoy perpetual tropical weather. In fact, Argentina, Chile, Paraguay, and Uruguay have temperate, multi-season climates. Winters are snowy, especially on the very southern tip of the continent. The seasons, however, are the reverse of seasons above the equator. So, if you want to escape the winter in the United States or Canada, just head down to Argentina in February. But if you go there in August, remember to take your skis and snow jacket.

Empires and
Conquest: A Look at
the History of the
Americas

Cerro Rico ("Rich Mountain") has generated unbe-
lievable amounts of wealth from its silver deposits—as
well as a terrible cost in death and suffering. The enormous
cone-shaped hill towers above the city of Potosí in Bolivia, and
for five hundred years, Cerro Rico has been tunneled by swarms
of "beetles," Native Indian and African mine workers. More than
eight million have died from the deadly conditions in Cerro Rico's silver
mines. In its heyday, the mine generated so much wealth that the Spanish
said they could build a bridge of silver stretching from South America clear
to Europe. Others have said that a bridge of bones could be built for the
same distance from all the workers who died working the mines.

colonization: the act of establishing new colonies.

smelted: melted ore to get metal from it.

galleons: large three-masted sailing ships used by the Spanish between the fifteenth and eighteenth centuries.

Renaissance: a period of cultural and artistic change lasting from about the fourteenth through the sixteenth centuries and signaling the end of the Middle Ages.

inflation: a period of an increase in the money supply without an increase in the supply of goods and services, leading to an increase in prices; too much money chasing too few goods.

iners extracted so much silver from Cerro Rico that the mine is said to have paid for Spain's *colonization* of the Americas. By the middle of the seventeenth century, silver exports represented 99 percent of all mineral exports from South America. The continent's silver was *smelted* in thousands of small ovens and carried by llama caravans to ports in Peru and Chile. Wooden *galleons* weighed down with precious metals sailed regularly from South American ports to Spain.

Not all the silver arrived. Untold amounts of wealth fell into the hands of the pirates of the Caribbean. But enough silver from Potosí arrived in Spain to pay for the extravagant culture of Spain's *Renaissance*. These riches from far away built the famous fleet called Spanish Armada and paid for wars fought by Spain against the Turks, Italians, Flemish, French, and English. It also caused runaway *inflation* and put many Spanish businesses out of work.

The wealthy and elegant town of Potosí was built beneath Cerro Rico, and an Indian named Diego Hualpa discovered the silver lode there in 1544. The census of 1573 said the population of Potosí was 120,000 inhabitants, more people than lived in Seville, Madrid, Rome, or Paris, and the same population as London at that time. Potosí was one of the largest and richest cities in the world—but the profits from all that silver went to a small group of European conquerors.

Meanwhile, the vast majority of Potosí's inhabitants were Indian and African slaves who were forced to work in the mines. These miners ate, slept, and worked underground for four

Peruvians used llamas for transportation.

The Uncle

Although the Spanish named it Cerro Rico, Potosí natives have another name for the mountain: "*El Tío*" (The Uncle). El Tío is the spirit of the mountain, portrayed as having a goat's beard, sharp horns, and red skin like *El Diablo* (the Devil), an appropriate image for a place that offers such temptation and causes so much suffering. Even today, Native miners make offerings of precious coca leaves to satisfy El Tío before they begin their labor in the mine shafts.

months at a time. Poisonous gasses and lung diseases killed them, on average, after they had worked in the mines only ten years.

Thousands of *coca-leaf*–chewing Indian miners still work the tunnels inside Cerro Rico. Miners labor more than eight hours a day, yet they make only $75 to $125 (U.S. dollars) each month. They still die early from the dreaded miners' disease *silicosis pneumonia*.

A Heritage of Oppression

he Spanish conquerors who ruled Potosí set up a pattern for Bolivia's society that to a large extent continues today. People of European heritage dominate the society, while poorer Native people struggle to make ends meet. Indigenous (Native) people speak either Quechua or Aymara languages. They live in mud houses and raise meager crops on dry lands. They may not be able to speak Spanish; in fact, less than half of Bolivians speak the official national language. Richer Bolivians tend to be *mestizos* (people of mixed European and Indian blood) living in the cities. They control Bolivia's wealth of natural resources.

Symbol for a Continent

he story of Cerro Rico could serve as a symbol for the history of all of South America. The continent's story involves European conquerors and Native people forced to work for them. It revolves around great material resources and nations where most of the poor struggle in poverty.

When Europeans arrived in the Western Hemisphere, it was already inhabited by hundreds of cultures, with a vast variety of languages, customs, and spiritual beliefs. No one knows for sure how many people lived in the Americas before Europeans ar-

coca-leaf: from the coca plant, it is dried and chewed as a stimulant or processed for cocaine.

silicosis pneumonia: a chronic lung disease caused by extensive exposure to silica dust.

Cerro Rico early in the twentieth century

29

Cutting the Earth in Half

I f you could divide our earth by cutting it in half from top to bottom, you would have two hemispheres (*hemi* means half, so a hemisphere is half of the globe). The Eastern Hemisphere contains Africa, Australia, Europe, and Asia. The Western Hemisphere holds what we today call the "Americas." This includes North America (Canada, the United States, and Mexico), Central America, and South America. For more than 10,000 years people who lived in the two halves of the world were totally unaware that the other half existed.

rived, but scholars guess between 40 and 90 million people inhabited the Western Hemisphere.

People who called themselves Runa lived throughout what is today known as South America. Before Westerners came, these people had developed a mighty empire. They regarded their king—the Inca—as the descendant of supernatural heroes. Their entire empire became known by the name of their ruler, so they too were called "Inca."

The Inca Empire was one of great and marvelous achievement. Cuzco, the Inca's capital, was an architectural wonder. The Runa carved enormous pictures of giant creatures—spiders, jaguars, and monkeys—on the Nazca Plains. These are so huge that their forms can only be recognized from the sky. Machu Picchu, the Inca's hidden mountain fortress, continues to amaze tourists who travel from around the world to see it.

First Contact

ontact between the two hemispheres began in South America in 1498, when Christopher Columbus sailed into the Gulf of Paria, which is today part of Venezuela. Reading ancient Greek scholars and religious texts had convinced Columbus that the Orient could be reached by sailing across the Atlantic Ocean. Muslim conquests had cut off trade routes to the East, so Europe was facing intense economic pressure to open up a new route. Columbus believed God had chosen him to find a route to the Orient in order to bring the wealth of the East home to Spain and to spread the Catholic religion to foreign lands. To the day he died, Columbus believed he had reached the Orient. He called the Caribbean and South American lands "the Indies" and the inhabitants "Indians."

From the beginning, Europeans saw Native Americans as fulfillment for their selfish wishes. Columbus assumed they would willingly serve Spanish masters and took some back to Spain as slaves. Europeans regarded the "New World" as theirs by right of discovery, and the *Pope* quickly confirmed this. Few Europeans ever considered the fact that these continents were already filled with people who should have been respected as the owners of their own lands. For the Natives of the Americas, contact with Europe was the beginning of a long battle for cultural

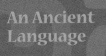

Pope: the head of the Catholic Church.

An Ancient Language

Many of the Inca's descendants continue to speak their ancestral language, Quechua, in South America today.

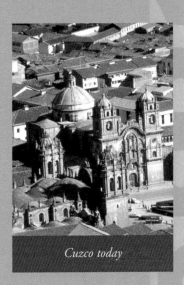

Cuzco today

Giant pictures carved on the Nazca Plains of Peru

survival that continues today. No one knows for sure how many Natives lost their lives as a result of European contact, but in the first hundred years, as many as 40 million Indians died from the results of disease, slavery, and slaughter.

For the Runa Empire, the Spanish invasion came at the worst possible time. Their entire culture was centered on their king, the Inca. Just before the Spanish arrived, the dying emperor Inca Capac couldn't decide which of his two sons should rule the empire after him, and a bloody civil war divided the empire. One brother, Inca Atahuallpa, had just won and was still finishing off his dead brother's forces when Spanish soldiers under the command of Francisco Pizarro marched into Peru.

F rancisco Pizarro was ruthless. He personally tortured Native leaders to make them tell him where he could find gold. One man who knew him said, "Committing cruelties against the Indians was a habit Pizarro knew by heart."

On November 14, 1532, Pizarro's forces arrived at the town of Cajamarca. Inca Atahuallpa met the Spaniards outside the town and told them to enter the city and wait for him there. Pizarro did so—and took advantage of the wait by preparing an ambush. The Inca and his officials arrived and spoke briefly through an interpreter with the Spaniards. The Indians clearly had no intention of surrendering, and so the Europeans sprang their trap. An Inca later recalled, "They could not get out, nor did they have any weapons—and the Spanish killed them all just as one would slaughter llamas, for nobody could defend himself."

Inca Atahuallpa was captured, and women taken in the ambush were raped. Pizarro demanded gold to ransom the emperor. The Natives delivered the gold—seven tons of it—but the Spanish had no intention of setting their hostage free. The Spaniards eventually killed Inca Atahuallpa by strangling him.

Warfare between the Spaniards and the Incas lasted another forty years, during which time more and more European invaders arrived. Atahuallpa's successor, Inca Manco, led his people against the Spanish for many years, but eventually, he was killed in an ambush.

And what became of the cruel conquistador who led in the conquest of the Inca Empire? As governor of conquered Peru,

Inca Manco's Wisdom

I nca Manco understood his enemy. He once told his countrymen, "Even if all the snow in the Andes turned to gold, still they [the Spanish] would not be satisfied." Before he was killed, Inca Manco told his people, "Reflect on how long my ancestors and I have looked after you . . . do not forget us, not in your lifetimes, not in the times of your descendants . . . do not forget our ceremonies." Though outwardly Catholic, many Incas today continue to practice their ancient traditions. After four centuries of European rule, their hearts still follow the Inca.

Francisco Pizarro never tried to restrain his fellow Spaniards' brutal treatment of the Indians. At the end of his life, however, after he was mortally wounded in a street fight between political parties, Pizarro made the sign of a cross with his fingers and begged to finally confess his sins. His attacker smashed an urn full of water on Pizarro's hand, and shouted, "In hell—you will have to confess in hell!" Pizarro died without the blessing of the Church, but his bones lie in an elaborate tomb in Lima Cathedral.

ore and more fortune-seekers came from Spain and Portugal to *exploit* the riches of South America. The Spanish remained focused on gold and silver, while the Portuguese established large plantations to grow sugarcane and tobacco, which were also shipped back to Europe. In some places, such as Argentina, so many Native people were killed that the conquerors ran short of slaves, fueling the slave trade from Africa.

Between 1492 and 1820, Europeans captured between 10 and 15 million Africans, packed them into foul compartments below the decks of slave ships, and sold them for labor in the Americas. Not all slaves were captured by Europeans, however; Africans often captured and forced other Africans into slavery in exchange for trade goods and military support from the European nations. The human cargo that was shipped to South America were the ancestors of the black populations in portions of the continent today.

Francisco Pizarro

These Native men in Ecuador speak Quechua.

As the conquistadors exhausted the deposits of silver and gold, they turned to other ways of making money; ranching became more and more important. South America was divided into *encomiendas*, ranches that were run like the plantations in America's South before the Civil War. Wealthy Europeans each had their own tracts of land, and the Indians who lived on that land were considered property of the landowners. In theory, the owners were expected to care for their workers. In practice, many Europeans treated the Natives like slaves; they were brutally worked, barely fed, and their women raped.

A Quechua woman in Bolivia

Racial Mixtures

here's a saying, "Columbus landed in 1492, and nine months later the first *Latinoamericano* was born." In many cases, pregnancies were the result of rape—but other unions between the races were lasting and tender. As a result, today's South Americans are a diverse racial mix. Some are predominantly European in their features, but the majority are mestizo—a mixture of European and Native. Many are of African heritage, and some have Asian backgrounds.

Los Indios—indigenous people such as the Inca—still make up a large portion of the population in parts of South America. Quechua (pronounced "kaitch-wa"), the language of the Inca Empire, is still spoken by approximately 13 million people in Bolivia, Peru, Ecuador, northern Chile, Argentina, and southern Colombia. Many native people in the highlands of the Andes live in ways remarkably similar to those of their ancient ances-

liberationists: those in favor of freedom.

tors. Sadly, indigenous people in South American countries also still face considerable prejudice. As Alan Cullison writes in *The South Americans*, "They understandably find economic opportunities scant on a continent where in places the popular word for Indian remains *chancho* (pig)."

Independence

n the nineteenth century, the nations of South America achieved independence from Europe. Two great heroes—Venezuela's General Simón de Bolívar and Argentina's General José de San Martín—led the battles for independence, Bolívar in the modern-day nations of Bolivia, Peru, Colombia, Ecuador, and Venezuela, and San Martín in Argentina, Chile, and Peru.

Simón Bolívar was born to a wealthy family in Venezuela. He traveled to Europe as a teenager, where Napoleon Bonaparte and liberal French politics fascinated him. Returning to Venezuela, Bolívar devoted himself to the cause of liberation. By 1810, he had become general of the rebel army, and for nine years, the *liberationists* fought back and forth against Spain's armies. Then, in 1819, Bolívar led a daring raid across the Andes to surprise Spanish troops in Bogotá, the first in a series of dramatic military victories.

Bolívar found it was easier to win a war than to keep the peace. After the revolution succeeded, he devoted himself to the dream of a united South America. He attempted to pull together Grenada, Ecuador, and Venezuela into

Simón Bolívar

one nation: Gran Colombia. The military leaders of the revolution retained power and did not share common ambitions, however, so Bolívar's dream of a united South American nation proved to be impossible. He ended his life brokenhearted and disillusioned. Shortly before his death, he said, "Latin America is ungovernable. Those who have served the revolution have plowed the sea."

The Andes mountains

Years of War

hortly after independence was gained, South American nations began squabbling with each other. In 1825, Brazil and Argentina went to war over disputed borderland. They made peace by creating the nation of Uruguay as a buffer between them. Forty years later, however, war broke out again; almost half of Paraguay's population died when Argentina, Brazil, and Uruguay attacked it in the War of the Triple Alliance. Meanwhile, Chile fought Peru and Bolivia for control of mineral-rich areas along the Pacific Ocean.

One noted South American landmark came about as a declaration of peace between South American nations. In 1902, Argentina and Chile were about to go to war over a disputed boundary in the Andes Mountains—but Pope Leo XIII issued a call to Catholic nations to refrain from warring against one another. The governments of Argentina and

A Unique Nation

The history of Guyana shows how diverse the backgrounds and cultures of South American nations can be. The first inhabitants of this land on the northern Atlantic Coast of South America were Carib Indians. European settlement began in 1615, when the Dutch established a fort. The Dutch traded with the Indians and established sugar plantations, and they bought African slaves to work these plantations. Conflicts between the English and Dutch led to Britain gaining control of Guyana in 1796. In 1834, slavery was abolished. This forced plantation owners to seek new workers. The British solved the problem by shipping indentured workers from India. From 1846–1917, almost 250,000 East Indian laborers entered Guyana. Guyana achieved independence in 1966. Its history is reflected in the continuing use of English and East Indian languages.

Showing Them Who Is Boss

he political history of South America has at times been dominated by *caudillos*. The word literally means "chief" or "leader," but it has also taken on the sense of "strong man"—a certain type of uncompromising and dictatorial leader. During the time of encomiendas, the caudillo was owner and supreme ruler of his ranch—allowed by the government in Spain to do whatever he wished with the people who lived to serve him and his property.

After South American nations gained independence from colonial rule, the pattern of strong leadership continued. Officers who had fought for freedom from Europe continued to rule over the poor people in their nations. There was little difference between them and the former rulers.

Even in the twentieth century, this pattern of dictatorial leadership continued in South American nations. In

Argentina, Juan Domingo Perón, the husband of the famous Evita Perón, censored the press and brutally silenced opposition politicians. In Chile, General Augusto Pinochet imprisoned thousands of students, intellectuals, and opposition politicians. He may have murdered or kidnapped some 6,000 people. The colonial heritage of caudillos has made it difficult for South American nations to form smooth-running democracies.

Chile listened. They asked diplomats from England and the United States to help them reach an agreement. *Christ of the Andes*, a twenty-six-foot (7.92 meters) tall bronze statue of Jesus commemorates their agreement—and the avoidance of war. Dedicated in 1904, it stands on the Argentine-Chilean border, bearing the Spanish inscription: "Sooner shall these mountains crumble into dust than Argentines and Chileans break the peace sworn at the feet of Christ the Redeemer."

Many South American countries experienced political and economic struggles during the twentieth century. Following a pattern set by the conquest, they continued to rely on export crops to support their economies. At times during the past century, this practice led to considerable economic growth. At other times, when demand for certain products dropped in the world market, it led to dire poverty and even political collapse. Military takeovers occurred in most of the major South American countries: Brazil in 1964, Uruguay in 1973, Chile in 1973, and Argentina in 1976. In its 175-year history, Bolivia has had 191 governments and sixty-two presidents. (Contrast that with thirty-seven presidents in the United States during the same time period.)

Economic hardships and the great gap between rich and poor have also led to riots and guerrilla warfare in some South American nations. During the 1980s, Peruvian

Peruvians, like other South Americans, have a long history of both cultural wealth and oppression.

Communist rebels known as the *Sendero Luminoso* (Shining Path) were responsible for more than 10,000 deaths. In Colombia, civil war between the FARC liberation army—increasingly allied with drug smugglers—and the national army has blighted the nation.

Communist: one who believes in the philosophy characterized by the belief in a classless society in which ownership and control of wealth and property goes to the state.

he history of South America is a grand drama, full of bravery and sacrifice, as well as greed and exploitation. The mixed heritage of Native, African, and European influences gives this continent an amazing diversity of cultural and human resources. At the same time, its history of conquest, oppression, and exported goods leaves South America with formidable challenges.

Many of its citizens have fled to the United States. As immigrants, they bring the resources of their rich cultural heritage with them—enriching North America as they do so.

⊞abla ⊞spañol

caudillo (cow-dee-ya): boss, leader, strong man

conquistador (cone-kees-tah-door): conqueror; a Spaniard who invaded America

45

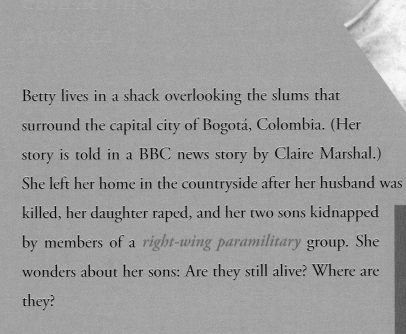

Betty lives in a shack overlooking the slums that surround the capital city of Bogotá, Colombia. (Her story is told in a BBC news story by Claire Marshal.) She left her home in the countryside after her husband was killed, her daughter raped, and her two sons kidnapped by members of a *right-wing paramilitary* group. She wonders about her sons: Are they still alive? Where are they?

right-wing paramilitary: a conservative group that uses military tactics although it is not part of the military.

47

left-wing: a member of a subgroup that is more liberal or radical than the rest of the group.

herbicides: poisons that kill plants.

She and her neighbors are victims of the civil war between *left-wing* rebels and right-wing forces allied with the government. Fearing more attacks, they chose to leave their farmlands and move in with more than two million people who live in dire poverty in the slums surrounding Bogotá.

She and other displaced women are trying to make the most of their situation. Dozens of desperately poor mothers come together in a tiny room where they share one decrepit sewing machine. They take turns using the machine to make clothes to sell—earning them at least a few desperately needed pesos.

Another Colombian family, Chairo, his wife Magola, and their three children, still live as farmers in the countryside, but their lives are becoming increasingly desperate. (Their story is told in a BBC report by Sue Branford.) They live in an area where many farmers grow coca, the plant that's the source for illegal drugs. The rebel forces pay farmers for coca and use profits from the drug trade to finance their war against the government. Chairo and his family did have one small crop of coca plants, but for the most part they were growing legal crops to sell and provide for the family.

One morning, they were surprised by government airplanes that flew overhead dumping *herbicides* onto their fields. "We watched as they sprayed everything in sight. All my crops were destroyed. The poison even got into the soil," Chairo said. The herbicides are so poisonous that it went deep into the soil, making it infertile so no crops will grow in the future. Even worse, the crop-dusting harmed the health of Chairo's family. "Look at our daughter," said Magola. "It's her eighteenth birthday today. And all she can do is lie in the hammock. She's still got diarrhea and is passing blood."

Ironically, the only crops that survived the government's surprise spraying were the very crops the government wished to de-

A slum in Ecuador

Colorful fabrics are sewn by South American women to earn money to support their families.

A farmer's home in the Andes

stroy; the few coca plants in Chairo's fields continue to thrive in the otherwise infertile soil.

Drugs and Poverty

he United States spends billions of dollars aiding the Colombian government in its efforts to fight leftist rebels and destroy the production of cocaine. At the same time, the United States has pressured Colombia to try and discourage Colombians from migrating illegally into the United States. Yet farmers like Chairo say the government's efforts are pushing them out of their traditional homes and forcing them to make desperate choices.

With his soil poisoned, what can Chairo and his family do? They could grow the hardiest and most profitable crop available to them, coca. By doing so, however, they risk even more pressure from the government. They could join the rebel forces, who would protect them from the government, but they are not comfortable siding with a group that is profiting so much from the addictions of people in other countries. They could move to the slums around the capital, but how will they live?

Or they could do what thousands of their fellow Colombian citizens have done—head for the United States with the hope of beginning a new life there. It may be that U.S. policies in Colombia are forcing the very migrations that American officials say they want to prevent.

A South American farm

A Heritage of Oppression

ecause of the patterns set in the past, some South American nations have found it difficult to create democratic, prosperous, and healthy lives for their people. The heritage of caudillo leadership has made democracy difficult. Military coups (government takeovers), violent revolutions, civil wars, and dictatorships have caused many middle-class South Americans to leave their homelands and seek safer haven in the United States.

51

The flag of Argentina

Prejudice against indigenous people and lack of economic opportunities in the countryside have caused great numbers of poor people to crowd South America's cities, also encouraging migration north. Women's rights in South America lag behind those of their North American sisters. Minority groups often lack legal protection and opportunities for advancement. For all these reasons, South Americans may find themselves seeking a new life in America.

Argentina

In the latter half of the twentieth century, the policies of dictator Juan Perón of Argentina caused many to migrate to the United States. Perón came into office promising to support the *descamisados*—the shirtless poor of Argentina—with new economic improvements. He did improve the industries of Argentina by borrowing money from Chile, Paraguay, Ecuador, and the United States. Unfortunately, the money created by this economic improvement was used to make members of the ruling party even wealthier.

Perón was able to gain popular support and be elected into office in part due to the popularity of his mistress, the actress Eva (commonly known as "Evita") Duarte. Evita's celebrity status brought Perón the support of workers and union members, and his marriage to Evita helped solidify Juan Perón's position. Evita made a great show of giving to the poor, establishing hospitals, and other kind deeds. She was an odd combination—partly a glamorous sex symbol, yet partly revered as a religious saint. The masses adored her.

Even Evita's charm, however, could not mask the dark side of Juan Perón's dictatorial rule over Argentina. Under Perón, the arrest, torture, and murder of political opponents became an almost daily routine. Some 30,000 Argentinean citizens "disappeared" under his rule. After Evita died of cancer, Perón married a dancer named Isabel, who served as his vice president during Perón's second term. Without Evita, and with public outcry rising against his oppressive policies, Perón lost public support. He did enjoy a brief return to power in 1973.

After Perón's reign ended, the people of Argentina faced economic woes. Through the 1980s the country experienced a 1,000 percent rise in inflation. The Perón dictatorship and economic trials of Argentina caused many Argentineans to leave the country, with the majority heading to the United States. One in five immigrants from Argentina settled in New York City, and another large group established a community in Miami, Florida.

Socialist: someone who believes in the theory that the means of production and distribution should belong to the people and operated fairly rather than based on market principles.

Chile

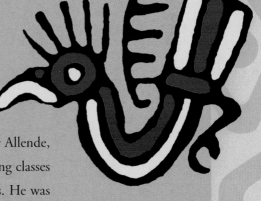

uring the 1970s, political turmoil in Chile also fueled flights to the United States. Salvador Allende, Chile's president, was a *Socialist*, elected by the working classes against the wishes of the military and wealthy citizens. He was also a friend of Fidel Castro, which led to fears of Chile becoming a Communist state. In September 1973, the military attacked the presidential palace. Allende either committed suicide or was killed—it is not certain what actually took place—and his government was overthrown. The United States Central Intelligence Agency (CIA) supported the coup.

After Allende was "removed," General Augusto Pinochet assumed power over Chile and ruled as a dictator for the next fifteen years. During that time, he was responsible for the murders of some 6,000 Chileans. An estimated one million people fled the country during those years, and many moved to the United States. In collaboration with Argentina, Paraguay, and Uruguay, Pinochet ran Operation Condor, which hunted down and forcibly returned Chileans who had fled to safety in other South American countries. Once back in Chile, they were tortured and executed.

During the Pinochet years, many Chileans became landless peasants. These moved into the "*villas callampas*" (mushroom towns), which grew quickly around Chile's large cities. Disease was rampant, and unemployment was around 80 percent for the people who lived in these communities.

In 1988, growing opposition in Chile combined with the withdrawal of U.S. support, causing Pinochet to be removed from office. Since then, there have been repeated efforts to bring the former leader to trial for crimes against humanity during his time in office. In 1998, he was arrested in Britain, at Spain's request. In 2000, he was allowed to return to Chile. Two years later, he was judged to be unfit for trial, due to failing health, but in 2004, he was stripped of legal immunity—opening the possibility that the eighty-eight-year-old former dictator may yet be brought to trial.

After Pinochet stepped down, many of those who had fled his regime returned to Chile to rebuild their suffering nation. Almost 100,000 remain in the United States, however, mostly living in New York City and in California.

n the 1980s, guerrilla activity in Peru caused some citizens to leave their country. During those years, the Shining Path (*Sendero Luminoso* in Spanish) conducted bombings, kidnappings, and open warfare in order to bring about a Communist revolution. Estimates vary, but as many as 30,000 Peruvians may have been killed in the conflict. The

Family View of a Coup

The niece of Salvador Allende is an internationally famous author, Isabel Allende. In her novel *House of the Spirits*, she describes the final attack on the presidential palace:

> By two o'clock in the afternoon the fire had consumed the old drawing rooms that had been left since colonial times and only a handful of men were left around the president. Soldiers entered the building. . . . Above the din was heard the hysterical voice of an officer ordering (the President's men) to surrender and come down in single file with their hands on their heads. The President shook each of them by hand. . . . They never saw him again alive.

rebels won control of large areas in the Peruvian mountains. They also terrorized residents in the capital. Some even feared that the Senderos might succeed in taking over the country.

The worst single incident occurred in July 1992, when two car bombs went off in the middle-class district of Miraflores, killing twenty people and injuring more than 250 others. Just two months later, however, the government dealt a decisive blow to the Shining Path rebels. The movement's founder, Abimael Guzman, was arrested in Lima along with six other rebel leaders. He was tried by a military court and sentenced to life imprisonment.

During the same time that the country was at war with the Communist guerrillas, Peru's economy took a nosedive. Inflation increased 1,700 percent. Peruvian money had so little value that it would take an entire suitcase full of bills to pay for a motel room for one night. During the 1980s, half a million Peruvians migrated to the United States. Most of these live today in New York, Illinois, and Florida.

Ecuador

A park in Miraflores, Peru

long with Colombia and Peru, the nation of Ecuador is the source of an especially large number of immigrants to the United States. This may be due to the continuing inability of the country to achieve economic or political stability. A very few rich citizens own the vast majority of Ecuador's wealth, while a small middle class struggles to survive. More than half of the Ecuadorian population lives at or below the

Ecuadorian money

poverty level. Changing international oil prices and tragic losses from flooding and volcanic eruptions, along with governmental mismanagement, have foiled the country's attempts to create a stable economy. Ecuador has had a democratically elected government since 1979, but it has been phenomenally unstable. On average, every two years a new civilian or military government takes control. This constant change has made it all but impossible for the government to help the country solve its economic problems. Prices and wages go up and down all the time. As one person who had lived in Ecuador put it, "It seems that just when something is about to change for the better, the country enters a period of economic decline." No wonder, with such pessimistic expectations for the fu-

The colors of a South American street

ture, that 281,000 Ecuadorians over the past three decades have made the difficult transition to a new life in the United States.

t the start of the twenty-first century, Venezuela has experienced considerable political turmoil. The Carter Center describes the crisis in Venezuela:

Growing poverty and plummeting confidence in the traditional political parties led to the election of Lt. Col. Hugo Chavez as president in 1998. . . . Despite early approval ratings exceeding 80 percent, his leadership style was confrontational, and the country became extremely divided and polarized, culminating in an attempted coup against him in April

A street person in South America

2002. He was removed from office by the military, until the military reversed course under pressure from other Latin leaders and from the people on the street, and put him back in office two days later.

President Chavez then asked the Carter Center to mediate (serve as a go-between) in discussions with the opposition. In May 2003, Chavez and his opposition agreed to a national *referendum* that would determine whether or not the President would remain in office. That vote took place in August 2004, with a clear margin voting to keep Chavez.

The vote should help to steady the situation in Venezuela, but the nation continues to be deeply divided. Observers fear that violence could happen again, as it did during the 2002 coup. A great divide exists between the lives of rich and poor in Venezuela. Chavez has a strong following among the poor, who

referendum: a vote by the entire population on a particular issue.

Venezuelan money

are the majority of voters. This is because he has poured money from the state-run oil monopoly into health, education, and food programs. Critics are concerned that Chavez might use his referendum victory to assume dictator-style control of the country. The Venezuelan Congress, dominated by Chavez supporters, recently approved a measure allowing that body to remove and appoint judges to the Supreme Court. The government also wants to control TV and radio stations that are critical of Chavez. The President has another plan to unite local police forces into a unified national force, which would give the national government more power.

During the 2002 crisis, *Miami Hurricane* newspaper reporter Danielle Scott reported on how events back home affected Venezuelan students studying in the United States. She interviewed Cristina Vanessa Vila, a freshman from Anzoatequi, Venezuela, who described her concerns during the crisis: "People are locked up in their houses and they're afraid. There are riots and civil war and they're just killing people. It's affecting the people in every possible way."

If Venezuela can resolve its deep political divisions peacefully, it will be welcome news for Venezuelans in their own nation, as well as for those living in the United States.

Flower sellers in a South American market

Habla Español

Los Estados Unidos (loce ace-tah-dohs oo-nee-dohs): the United States

revolución (ray-vo-loo-see-own): revolution

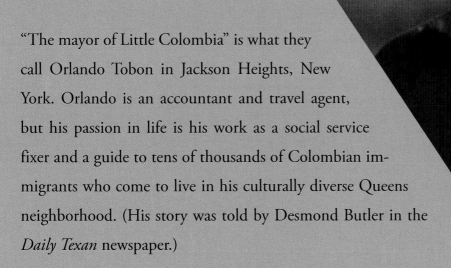

"The mayor of Little Colombia" is what they call Orlando Tobon in Jackson Heights, New York. Orlando is an accountant and travel agent, but his passion in life is his work as a social service fixer and a guide to tens of thousands of Colombian immigrants who come to live in his culturally diverse Queens neighborhood. (His story was told by Desmond Butler in the *Daily Texan* newspaper.)

In 1968, at age seventeen, Tobon came to New York with only $60 to his name. He earned a degree in accounting while working several menial jobs and later started Orlando Travel, a travel agency and tax accounting business. Soon Orlando was not only consulting on tax returns but on everything else as well. He takes care of clients and people with problems, sorting their documents, giving advice, and working on their behalf with the Internal Revenue Service.

"The undertaker of the mules" is another name people have called Tobon. "Mules" is a slang term for immigrants recruited by drug traffickers to carry illegal drugs into the United States. Orlando Tobon has helped dozens of Colombian families get back the remains of members who died smuggling drugs into New York. Some mules have ended up on the wrong side of drug gangs, and others have died when drug-filled capsules wrapped in condoms burst in their stomachs.

Julio Olarte knew where to turn after his sister Tatiana was found dead in a local hotel from a burst drug capsule. Olarte was not able to pay $2,500 to the mortuary to claim his sister's body, and the city would bury the body if it wasn't claimed. Tobon began raising money within the community so that Olarte would be able to bury his sister with dignity.

This was not the first time Tobon had helped the Olarte family. Twenty-two years ago, Julio's mother was not allowed to board a plane from Bogotá to New York because she was in the final stages of pregnancy. Her husband made a call to Tobon, who fixed the problem with a call to a friend at the Colombian airline, Avianca—and so Julio Olarte was born in America.

Immigrants appreciate the help of people like Orlando Tobon because it is difficult to make the adjustments between life in one nation and life in another. For many immigrants, settling into communities such as Jackson Heights, with its estab-

Many South Americans find it difficult to escape poverty and oppression.

Immigrants settling into this Queens, New York, neighborhood will face many challenges.

New immigrants receive help from many agencies.

lished South American immigrant community, has advantages. Many South American immigrants fear the immensity of North American cities and the very different culture where few speak Spanish. They are drawn to areas where other South Americans live. Even with the comfort of their own people surrounding them, however, the challenges of learning a new language, maintaining their own culture while adjusting to a new one, and many more issues confront South American immigrants.

s you read this book, some South American is probably waiting to hear his name called at an embassy to start the immigration process. Many times this part of the journey is the most difficult. In some countries, such as Colombia, one may have to wait as long as three years for an appointment with the consulate just to start the application process. The fee to set up a consulate appointment is $65.

Once a person has the consulate appointment, the next important step is to get a visa. There are two types of visas: immigrant visas and nonimmigrant visas. The first is for people who want to stay in the United States permanently. Nonimmigrant visas are for students, businesspeople on a business trip, tourists, people needing medical treatment, and highly skilled professionals contracted for specific temporary jobs. A visa will cost $260. The U.S. State Department classifies immigrants as either "unlimited immigrants" or "limited immigrants." No restrictions are placed on the people in the first category for entering into the United States. Unlimited immigrants include:

- American citizens
- people married to American citizens
- widows or widowers of American citizens
- parents of American citizens
- legal U.S. residents (green card holders)

Limited immigrants need to have a legal resident sponsor them or must have a job offer in order to enter the United States. The categories for an employment-based visa include the following:

- internationally recognized artists, athletes, businesspeople, professors, and scientists
- executives and managers of American companies

- professionals holding advanced degrees
- highly skilled workers of jobs and professions requiring at least two years of experience and training
- seasonal workers who come and go each year

The State Department prioritizes visas based on employment or family relations. Children of American citizens are given first preference. Second preference is given to a wife or husband and unmarried child of a permanent resident alien. Third are the spouses of the children of U.S. citizens. Last in line are the siblings of U.S. citizens.

Once a person has a visa, she has up to six months to make traveling arrangements. She needs to have enough money to cover the cost of the trip as well as enough money for the move once she reaches her destination. For individuals with higher incomes, this may not be a problem, but many South Americans have an average monthly salary that's less than $100.

The United States also limits the number of immigrants allowed to enter the country every year. America's "worldwide limitations" are as follows:

1. 366,000 family-sponsored immigrants
2. 123,291 employment-based immigrants.
3. Only seven percent of the immigrants may come from each nation per year.

A lottery is held every year in the United States called "the Diversity Lottery" or the "Green Card Lottery." This lottery grants visas to 55,000 randomly selected prospective immigrants. If someone wins this lottery, he is not required to have family already in this country nor an employment opportunity

South American women offer each other practical and emotional support.

in place. Most people in Latin America can apply for a winning lottery ticket, unless they come from countries that already have many immigrants in the United States, such as Colombia, the Dominican Republic, El Salvador, and Mexico. Lottery participants must be high school graduates, have two years of work experience in a profession that requires training, and must meet the regular requirements for getting a visa. Entrants write their name and date of birth on a piece of paper, include a photograph, and mail it to the National Visa Center in Kentucky.

The U.S. government makes a distinction between economic and political immigrants. Economic immigrants choose to leave their country to lead a better life in the United States; theirs is a voluntary immigration. Political immigrants are seeking safety from political persecution in their own country; they see themselves as leaving the better life behind.

Regardless of the reason for entering the country, once an immigrant is here, there are two ways she can remain in the United States: become a permanent resident by obtaining a green card, or become a naturalized citizen. An immigrant can apply for a green card—which is not actually green—after he has been in the United States for three years. The official name of this card is the Alien Registration Green Card and it must be carried at all times. The cardholder must pay taxes and can be drafted into the armed forces. Once a person has a green card, she is a permanent resident and is allowed to stay in the United States for as long as she wants. She can freely leave the country and return once she has a green card. She has the same rights as citizens except for the right to vote.

After two years of possessing a green card, an immigrant can apply for citizenship if he meets the following requirements:

- speaks English (this may be waived if the person is over a certain age)
- is at least eighteen years of age
- demonstrates he has lived in the United States for five years or more
- has no criminal record
- shows knowledge of American institutions, history, and culture

A judge must interview the applicants. If the judge recommends that the immigrant can become a naturalized citizen, he participates in a public ceremony swearing allegiance to the United States. The right to vote is now given; unless he is found to have lied on his application or commited a major act against the United States, no one can ever take away his citizenship.

A woman from South America will face many challenges as she journeys to the United States.

South American children playing together

hether an immigrant becomes a permanent resident or a citizen, she will have many adjustments to make once she is in North America. For example, when Maruja (María) Lander, a Peruvian, came to Binghamton, New York, with her British husband in 1984, her biggest hardship was the language barrier. Her two young children were in a preschool, and Maruja found the experience of not being able to communicate with the teacher to be painful. How could she find out how her children's day had gone or if there were any problems? Maruja was delighted to make friends with a neighbor who had children close in age to hers. After some weeks, however, the neighbor became very cold and unfriendly and no longer invited the Lander children over to play. Maruja had no idea what had happened. She wondered if she had offended the neighbor in some way, but she could not find out because of the language difference. Eventually, Maruja found a free

A Peruvian girl

English-as-a-Second-Language (ESL) class in Binghamton, and this class was the greatest help to her during that first year. The teacher was warm and supportive, and Maruja learned how to communicate in English.

A professor of math with a master's degree in her own country, Maruja decided to make a career change. She went back to school, got her master's in computer science, and landed a job with IBM as a computer programmer. Later, she found she missed teaching college students and jumped at the opportunity to join a community college's faculty as a math and computer instructor. Maruja remembers feeling insecure about her English for her first year as an instructor, but she slowly gained confidence.

Racism is not something Maruja has felt in this country. Her South American friends in town feel similarly. She notices that friends from Mexico and Central America feel more discriminated against.

Maruja believes that the greatest challenges to South American immigrants are the language barrier and the difficulty of obtaining a visa. Some immigrants come knowing no English and don't have employment. Not all are as fortunate as Maruja to be able to work in their previous professions; instead, many have to work at menial jobs for years—and

Older people may find the language barrier nearly impossible to bridge.

yet they faithfully send money back to families in South America. People who formerly worked as university professors may have to work as janitors, babysitters, and factory workers. Their lives can be very difficult.

ot knowing the language can cause difficulty in many areas of immigrants' lives. Deborah Kong relates the experience of Elvia Marin in *Colloquio Online*, the electronic newsletter of the Hispanic community of the Baltimore-Washington, D.C., area. Mr. Marin struggled in his halting English to express just how bad the pain in his wife's stomach and back was. It was worse than childbirth. He did not know the words that would have helped identify the problem—such as "urinary tract stones"—and the doctors in the emergency room couldn't identify the problem. The couple left the hospital untreated.

Many immigrants with little English-speaking abilities come into hospitals and doctors' offices. According to the American Medical Association, interpreter costs can range from $30 to $400, making it very expensive for doctors who say they want to help patients but object to the high costs. Doctors often rely on relatives, friends of patients, receptionists, and janitors to help interpret to patients.

"I felt really desperate and also frustrated at my inability to communicate in English and explain my own problem," said Marin, "I feel like we're not being listened to, not being paid attention to. We're not considered important." One immigrant patient who had no interpreter thought she was being kidnapped when she was driven a hundred miles from a clinic in Fresno, California, to one in Modesto.

The Wake Forest University School of Medicine is making an effort to help Latino immigrants. The school is the first to require students to learn Spanish under a new curriculum suggested by the students themselves. Sarah Cartwright, a recent graduate, stated, "When you can even speak some Spanish, you can really connect better with the patient."

Holding On to Cultural Heritage

any Latino immigrants wish to overcome the language barrier as quickly as possible, while at the same time remaining aloof from North America's culture. They do not wish to *assimilate* but to keep their rich cultural heritage. Alan Cullison speaks of this issue in his book *The South Americans*. He describes Geraldo Heredia, a Peruvian who settled in Connecticut, and who made sure he spoke Spanish with his children at home. His family joined a Peruvian club in town where his children learned the history of their original country. The family returned to Peru for vacations so the children could get to know the country. Geraldo's brothers, who all grew up in North America, married Peruvian wives whom they met while living in Connecticut.

Most South Americans admire North American technological progress and its system of democracy—but at the same time, they feel they have a distinctively different culture and worldview they want to keep. Americans may seem *materialistic* and one-sided to them. They feel that Latinos have better family values, are more well rounded, and have a higher appreciation for art and music than do most North Americans.

Alan Cullison tells of a Chilean immigrant, Rosa Tapias-Calpa. Rosa did not appreciate the American values taught in public schools, so she paid to have her girls educated in a Catholic school. She did not like the fact that in public schools girls were allowed to wear tight pants, and openly kiss boys. In Chile, the girls wear skirts to school and are not allowed to dis-

Maintaining their cultural heritage is a goal for many South American immigrants.

Evangelical: any
Protestant church whose
members believe in the
absolute authority of
the Bible and salvation
through the personal
acceptance of Jesus
Christ.

play such affection with the opposite sex. Rosa did not allow her daughters to go on dates without a chaperone or to go to movies. They were not allowed to play popular music. In spite of their careful upbringing, Tapias-Calpa believes her children are more like North Americans than Chileans: "I try to teach them my way but everything they learn is American."

n any given Sunday morning you will find many South Americans worshipping in a Catholic or *Evangelical* church. This is another way to help maintain their culture while at the same time receive help adjusting to a new life. Many years ago, the diocese of Brooklyn-Queens established the Spanish Apostolate. The Reverend René Valero, a Venezuelan priest, started the program and eventually had more than fifty Spanish-speaking priests. Today, the Spanish Apostolate still holds an important place in the lives of South Americans in New York City.

The church is often a place to foster culture as well as to serve as a bridge to North American culture. For example, Templo Calvario, in Los Angeles, California, the largest Hispanic Charismatic church in America, helps immigrants making the transition from their professions in their countries of origin to working in those same professions in America. At the church, immigrants learn English vocabulary for their jobs, as well as how to take the required examinations. This is a much-needed service, since the transition can be daunting and confusing.

Gender-Role Adjustments

O ne of the many adjustments that a female immigrant may need to make in North American society is the differing role of women. Many women here have a greater responsibility in earning a living. In some South American societies the women stay at home to raise the children, and the men are the breadwinners. In the video, *Transnational Fiesta: 1992*, Gareth Denhan told of the big adjustments to be made in his cross-cultural marriage to his Peruvian wife. She expected to do all of the household duties and expected him to make all of the family decisions.

Cultural Leaps

I magine the transition an immigrant from the highlands of Peru would experience coming to America. Whereas the majority of immigrants from South America come from a middle-class section of society, a group of Incan descendants from the large peasant community of Cabanaconde in the southern Peruvian Andes have settled in the Washington, D.C., area.

The Quispe family started the immigration process when one of their daughters took a position as a nanny with a Brazilian family who moved to Washington. After working with the family for some time, the Quispe daughter, seeing the great economic opportunities to be had in the United States, decided to remain in America and make a life for herself. She kept in contact with her family back in Cabanaconde, and eventually she convinced her parents along with most of her siblings to join her in America.

In the video titled *Transnational Fiesta: 1992*, the Quispe family talks of the difficulties and joys of living in America. All the siblings had to work at menial jobs when they first arrived in the country, but since then, some have gone to school and are now employed in better-paying jobs. The task of learning English was a difficult one for each member of the family. When asked if they felt like Americans yet, they said no, they are still very much Cabaños. One brother thought he would return someday to Cabanaconde. Gladys, one of the sisters, said she felt like an American when she was in the United States and a Cabeña when she was in Peru. Most of the family members expect to stay in the United States.

The Quispe family all agree that their main reason for being here is the economy. Whereas in Peru they might have made $50 in a month, here they can make that much in an hour. The consensus between the family members is that Peru is in deep trouble economically, socially, culturally, and morally, and that they are better off in the United States. The family appreciates America's democratic system, but they also believe that American culture is lacking in some other ways. They see Americans as anti-family, distant from each other, cold, and not as caring as members of the Latino culture. The American lifestyle is frantic, with everyone trying to make more money, usually for frivolous things. The Quispes hope to keep their identity as Peruvian Cabeños with all their family values and good work ethics while still being an active community in the United States. Most South American immigrants express these same sentiments.

Where Are the South Americans in the United States?

ere are the ten states with the most South American immigrants:

- New York—518,251
- Florida—407,880
- New Jersey—238,123
- California—202,628
- Massachusetts—69,805
- Texas—66,623
- Virginia—51,570
- Connecticut—48,144
- Illinois—42,519
- Maryland—41,626

Habla Español

visado (vee-sah-doh): visa

migración (mee-grah-see-own): migration

Help from the Community

Sounds of music from the Peruvian Highlands float through the suburban Washington, D.C., night, and Latinos and North Americans dance to the rhythm. Later, women in colorful, multilayered skirts and embroidered jackets, topped in gray hats, whirl in traditional dances with men sporting white shirts, calf-length black pants tied with woven belts, and black hats. The evening is festive with music, laughter, and traditional foods from the village of Cabanaconde, a village high in the Andes of Peru.

A counselor at a Youth Co-op in Miami helps immigrants adjust to life in their new homes.

The Cabanaconde City Association (CCA) is sponsoring the event. "Our purpose is to help those arriving from Cabanaconde . . . offering them credit with the low interest that North American banks do not offer," said the CCA President when interviewed for the video *Transnational Fiesta: 1992*. More than three hundred immigrants have come from the little Peruvian village since the 1970s. The CCA was established in the mid-1980s and is one of the only officially recognized Peruvian migrant associations in the Washington, D.C., area. Cabeños feel that if it weren't for the association, they would not be such a close-knit group.

Helping Hands

A food pantry in Los Angeles lends a hand to struggling immigrants.

hankfully, the United States has many dedicated organizations that strive to make the transition for new immigrants seamless. One such group is the American Friends Service Committee (AFSC). During World War I, many young men from the religious group the Quakers—or Friends—were conscientious objectors (they did not believe it was right to kill another person even in war). The AFSC was started to give these men a chance to serve those in need instead of fighting. Today the group is very involved in many ways around the world; assisting immigrants is one of these. The AFSC now has fifty members working on immigration rights issues around the United States.

AFSC provides training and assistance in Newark, New Jersey, to two "asylee associations," the Action Network for Refugees and Asylum-seekers and QuIr: Queer Immigrant Rights, a group of lesbian, gay, bisexual, and transsexual asylees. (An asylee is a person already in the United States who is granted legal status due to a claim of persecution or feared persecution in his home country.) Every month these two associations meet to discuss information about housing, employment opportunities, and helpful ideas for living in the United States. Members are planning to bring attention to the community regarding the hardships caused by the ten- to twelve-year wait for asylees waiting to receive permanent residency cards or green cards.

In Stockton, California, the Rural Economic Alternatives Project gets support for new types of economic development, low-income housing, the participation of local immigrants in multi-ethnic events as well as other activities to strengthen the differing populations of ethnic people in California. In another California town, Visalia, Project Voice is working with college students and other young immigrants. The current project is to get support from the community for the Dream Act, a bill pending in the U.S. Congress to help *undocumented* students. If passed, the bill would allow these students who graduate from a U.S. high school to attend college, to be accepted for in-state tuition, and someday receive legal status. The participants are working in the community to get signatures to show support of the Dream Act. They are also speaking to various groups and are being helped by broadcasts publicized by Project Voice, on Radio Grito (Shout Radio).

Another organization that aids immigrants is the National Network for Immigrant and Refugee Rights (NNIRR). The purpose of NNIRR is to make sure that the United States has a just immigration and refugee policy. It also emphasizes the need to address issues internationally. Trying to build international support and cooperation to strengthen the safety, rights, and welfare of migrants and refugees is on the NNIRR agenda.

Building a Race and Immigration Dialogue in the Global Economy—also known as BRIDGE—is a project of NNIRR to help community organizers, activists, and educators take on issues related to immigrant and refugee rights. Based on two years of community input and testing, an exciting BRIDGE curriculum has been published. The BRIDGE project provides training, leadership development, and community education to immigrants.

Unloading food donated to Obras de Amor, a California agency that provides relief

Life in the United States can be both good and bad for immigrants.

or many South American immigrants, life in North America is very different from their old life. For those from Cabanaconde, Peru, the change from a 4,000-member peasant community to the megalopolis of Washington, D.C., is mind-boggling. Each immigrant must make tremendous leaps of adjustment—intellectually, socially, emotionally, and even spiritually.

When asked what she thought about North American society, one of the Quispe sisters remarked, "It's both good and bad. I like their way of life, how they try to help and relate to you." If the Quispes had lived among their Inca ancestors many years ago and happened upon a fellow citizen passing on the road, a common greeting would have been, "Oh child of the Sun, loving and kind to the poor!" Today not all immigrants are poor economically, but all are poor in the sense of being unsettled and needing assistance. Luckily, some North American organizations have seen the need and responded.

Habla Español

ayudar (ay-you-dahr): help

bienvenida (bee-ane-vane-ee-day): welcome

For many years there were no laws for immigration into North America, but in the mid-nineteenth century, immigration restrictions began to be made. Some were made for humanitarian reasons, while others were for the interests of the United States. For example, in 1910 after the destruction of the Mexican Revolution, over 700,000 Mexicans were allowed to flee to the United States. During World War II, the *Bracero* Program allowed 220,000 workers from Mexico to come and help replace the thousands of young American farmers who were enlisted to fight overseas. The following are some of the immigration acts of the 1900s:

- **Immigration Act of 1917**: Asia was banned from immigration. Before arriving in the United States, it was necessary for immigrants to take a literacy exam.

- **Immigration Act of 1924**: Under this act, only those nations that were already represented by officials in the United States were allowed to immigrate. Central and South America were included together in the quotas given to Spain. European immigrants were favored.

- **Immigration and Nationality Act of 1952**: Immigration from Asia was still banned. Quotas were given to countries accepted by the United Nations.

- **Immigration and Nationality Act of 1965**: Restrictions on Asia and Latin American immigrants were lifted as the national origin quotas were ended.

- **Immigration Act of 1990**: Professionals, people with particular talents and skills such as athletes and performers, and family-sponsored immigrants were given favored status.

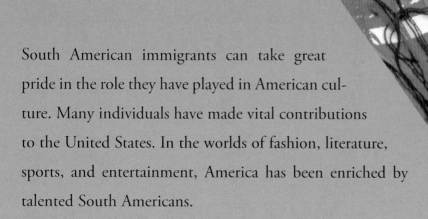

South American
Contributions to the
United States

South American immigrants can take great
pride in the role they have played in American culture. Many individuals have made vital contributions
to the United States. In the worlds of fashion, literature,
sports, and entertainment, America has been enriched by
talented South Americans.

Carolina Herrera

"Hispanic women have always had an incredible sense of style and elegance," declared Carolina Herrera (quoted in *Biographical Dictionary of Hispanic Americans* by Nicholas E. Meyer). She proved her point as she accepted the 1987 MODA award for Top Hispanic Designer.

Born María Carolina Josefina Pacanins in Caracas, Venezuela, in 1939, Herrera immigrated to New York where she has resided for many years. At age thirty, Carolina married Reinaldo de Herrera and two years later she was on the International Best-Dressed List. She was also named as one of the Ten Most Elegant women in the world by *Elle* magazine.

The clothes that Herrera began to make and design were well cut, graceful, and comfortable. Soon her rich and famous friends were convincing her to sell her creations. In 1981, she began her first line of clothes. Her company, *House of Herrera*, was known for sleek, elegant day wear and tasteful evening wear. The colors that Caroline leaned toward were black, white, and yellow. Seventeenth- and eighteenth-century Spanish clothing often inspired her.

Since she believes that taste is universal, Carolina's fashions appeal to people of all cultures and especially to many of the top names in U.S. social circles. Caroline Kennedy, daughter of the late president John F. Kennedy, contracted Herrera to design her wedding dress.

Carolina Herrera

Shakira

hakira Isabel Mebarak Ripoll was born February 9, 1977, in the Colombian city of Barranquilla. Her mother was Colombian and her father of Lebanese descent. The name Shakira comes from her Arabic father and means "woman full of grace."

Born into a poor family, Shakira absorbed music from both parents' cultures. She wrote her first song at age eight and soon began winning talent competitions. When she was eleven, she began taking guitar lessons—but she was kicked out of her school choir for singing too loudly. Shakira's family moved to Bogotá when she turned thirteen; they were hoping she could start a modeling career. Instead, she made a record deal with Sony's Colombian division. Her debut record album, *Magia* (Magic) came out in 1991.

From there, Shakira went on to record many other albums:

- *Peligro* (Danger): 1993
- *Pies Descalzos* (Barefeet): 1995; a number-one hit in eight countries and a platinum record in the United States.
- *Donde Esta Los Ladrones* (Where are the thieves): 1998; this album opened up the U.S. market to Latino music and was another platinum record.
- *MTV Unplugged*: 2000; topped the Latin charts for two weeks and became another platinum record. It won a Grammy for Best Latin Pop Album, and at the first Latin Grammy Awards ceremony in 2000, Shakira took home trophies for Best Female Pop vocal for "Ojos Asi" and Best Female Rock Vocal for "Octavo Dia" from this album.
- *Laundry Service*: 2001; Shakira's first almost-all-English album. "Whenever, Wherever" was a fantastic hit among English speakers. Almost immediately, *Laundry Service* was at number three on the North American pop charts. One year later, the album went triple platinum.

Shakira now makes her home in Miami, Florida, although she is an international star. She went on a world tour for almost two years and sang to sold-out audiences in many

Jaime Escalante

countries. *Time* chose Shakira as the cover photo in a recent issue with an article titled "Era of the Rockera." In Monaco, she won Latin Female Artist of the Year at the World Music Awards. The Colombian government designated her as an official goodwill ambassador. She even received an audience with the Pope in the Vatican. (Did the Pope tap a finger or two when he listened to this outstanding Latina artist?)

Jaime Escalante

aime Escalante was born on December 31, 1930, in La Paz, the capital of Bolivia. Born to a middle-class family, Jaime graduated from San Andrés University in La Paz and then taught science and mathematics at a military academy and two high schools in his native country. Jaime was greatly revered as a teacher in Bolivia, but he decided to leave for the United States to find a more stable life than he could find in his country at that time.

Like many immigrants, Jaime had to return to school to earn his U.S. teaching credentials, since his Bolivian teaching credentials were not acknowledged and his English needed improvement. He threw himself into a whirlwind of menial jobs while pursuing the skills he needed. At the same time, he studied at Pasadena City College and then California State University in Los Angeles. He graduated with a B.S. degree in mathematics and was ready to teach by 1974.

The true story that follows was portrayed in a 1988 film, *Stand and Deliver*. Jaime could have his pick of jobs at this point of his life, but he remained true to his passion in life and pursued a teaching career. He chose a difficult path, but one that would do the most good in life, and became a teacher at Garfield High School in the Chicano barrio— a place where he would use the street language and knowledge he had acquired while working at humble jobs.

Because of their hard lives, many students at Garfield High were rebellious and uninterested in learning. Jaime was a determined educational warrior, though, and through compassion and persistence, he took his students from a low-level ability in math to good passing grades on a national advanced-placement calculus test. Only two percent of pupils in the United States even try this exam, so officials were so amazed by the students' scores that they suspected cheating. Under careful scrutiny, the students went on to make even higher grades on the re-take exam.

Among the awards given to Jaime are these: the White House Hispanic Heritage Award (1989), the Hispanic Engineer National Chairman's Award (1989), and the

American Institute for Public Service's Jefferson Award (1990). He is not only recognized in the United States but internationally as well. The media has acclaimed him as "an authentic American hero."

As a true hero, Jaime Escalante's greatest rewards have been the wonderful effects of his work. As the years have passed, many of his students have succeeded in passing the difficult advanced-placement calculus test and have gone on to colleges with scholarship offers. The icing on the cake is that many scholarship funds have been created in his honor.

Isabel Allende

ublishers have called Isabel Allende the most widely read Latin American novelist ever. She was born to Chilean parents living in Lima, Peru, on August 2, 1942. Her father was a diplomat with the Chilean embassy and was related to Salvador Allende, who was elected president of Chile in 1970. Allende spent her growing up years in Bolivia and Lebanon. When Isabel was a child, her father left the family, and her mother married another Chilean diplomat.

Throughout her adult life, Isabel wore many hats. She worked as a secretary for an agency for the United Nations in Chile, as a journalist and writer of children's literature, as a TV show host, as an editor of a juvenile magazine, and as a staff member of a woman's magazine that pioneered *feminism* in Chile.

In 1973, a long bloody period of military reign began in Chile. President Allende was either murdered or forced to commit suicide. Isabel expressed her outrage at his death at the funeral service of a well-known Chilean poet, Pablo Neruda, a Nobel Prize winner in literature. Her family was upset that she took such a risk to her safety, and she soon lost most of her jobs because of her reputation of being against the government. During the tumultuous years that followed, Isabel was involved in compassionate activities to aid victims of the new government—but these activities did nothing to make the government feel better about her. In 1975, in fear for their lives, she and her husband and children went into *exile* and lived in Venezuela for the next thirteen years.

Isabel Allende

Living in exile must have brought out the writer in Allende, for in 1982, at age forty, she published her first novel, *La Casa de los Espíritus* (*The House of the Spirits*)—her family history in fiction form. Two years later, she wrote a novel about people involved in mass political murders, based on true events in Chile—*De Amor y de Sombra* (*Of Love and Shadows*). Both books were internationally acclaimed and were made into motion pictures.

In 1987, Allende's novel *Eva Luna* was considered "one of the year's best books" by the U.S. publication *Library Journal*.

feminism: *the belief that women should be treated and have the same opportunities as men.*

exile: *unwilling absence from one's own country or home.*

Cuentos de Eva Luna (*Eva Luna's Stories*) was another book Isabel wrote, a popular selection of narratives. These books have been translated into twenty-five languages.

Isabel Allende now lives in San Francisco, California, where she teaches creative writing at the University of California. She visits her country of Chile, but she has chosen to stay in the United States.

Bob Burnquist

ost of us would get dizzy watching Bob Burnquist. He specializes in skateboarding, switch stance (backward). Born in Rio de Janiero on October 10, 1976, he began skating at age eleven.

In 1995, Bob, a newcomer to the skateboarding world, competed in the Slam City Jam in Vancouver, Canada. Although there were many champs there, Bob walked away with first-place status. Since then, he has won many awards and contests. Some of his awards include:

- ESPY nomination for Action Sports Person of the Year
- Laureus World Sports Award for Alternative Sports Person of the Year
- At the SPOT in Tampa, Florida, he was crowned the Ocean Pacific "King of Skate"

You can play Bob's character in Tony Hawk Pro Skater and X Games Skateboarding video games. You can see him on the cover for *Sports Illustrated for Kids* and many skateboarder magazines, and recently he has been drinking milk . . . for the *Got Milk* mustache ads. He is an endorser for some large companies such as Activision, Oakley, and Lego.

Bob now lives in Vista, California, but he has not forgotten his South American roots. Many see his strong determination and character as a role model for Brazilian youth.

Bob Burnquist

Habla Español

maestro/maestra (my-ace-troh/my-ace-trah): teacher (male and female)

cantar (con-tar): to sing

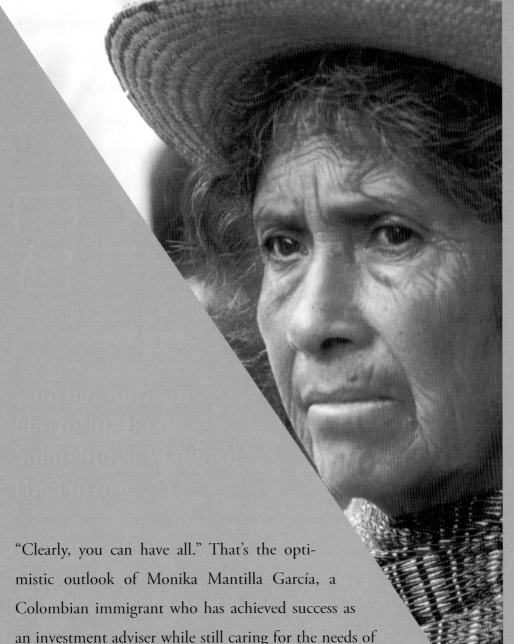

"Clearly, you can have all." That's the optimistic outlook of Monika Mantilla García, a Colombian immigrant who has achieved success as an investment adviser while still caring for the needs of her home. Eman Varoqua interviewed Mantilla for an article in *Hispanic Online* magazine. Mantilla is one busy woman—in the morning she can be found preparing the family breakfast while handling a conference call.

capital: money, property, and goods that can be used to create more wealth.

money markets: mutual funds that sell their shares to buy short-term securities and then convert the profits into additional shares for their shareholders.

Monika Mantilla García wants Latinas to know how wide the doors of opportunity can swing open for them. She believes they can have it all—a business career, a happy family, and a role in their Latino community. Mantilla began as a lawyer. She then earned an MBA from Columbia Business School in New York, married Juan Carlos García, an investment banker, and achieved a successful career in the investment world. Mantilla has been invited to speak at universities and before members of Congress. She also has a young daughter, Tatiana; Mantilla says Tatiana is her number-one priority.

Mantilla believes that the future looks bright for Latinos as they gain knowledge in the areas of investment and business. "We'll be able to raise our education levels, provide more opportunities to our community, and become a much more valuable community. But we need to have access to *capital*."

Mantilla works for Consultiva Internacional in New York, the only Latino investment management firm in the country. The firm helps 120 clients manage $2.5 billion. This is especially impressive considering that a recent study found less than two percent of the capital in *money markets* is managed by businesses that focus on minority communities. Mantilla believes there are "tremendous opportunities [for Hispanic advisers]. If you are able to provide quality, caliber, and experience, people will respect you." At the same time, she says, "To be in financial services we don't have to give up our roles as mothers, wives, or active community members. It's all about striking a balance." She admits that, "Sometimes it doesn't quite work out the way you plan, but you keep at it and you find your way." Increasingly, South American immigrants like Mantilla are finding their way toward greater happiness in the United States.

I t used to be said that the United States was a "melting pot"—a place where immigrants from many different cultures came together and melded into one new American identity. Today, we realize that America is more like a salad bowl, where each food retains its own unique identity. The lettuce does not become a tomato, and the tomato is distinct from the crouton or the dressing. In the same way, twenty-first century North America is like a salad: an enjoyable combination of people from a great variety of backgrounds. Each person keeps her own individual cultural identity—whether African American, American Indian, Asian, or South American—and yet each contributes to make the United States a creative and exciting nation.

By the year 2050, Latino Americans will number 80 million. The U.S. Census Bureau estimates that the white non-Hispanic population will grow about seven percent between 2000 and 2050, while the Hispanic population will increase by 194 percent. Shortly after that, non-Hispanic whites will become a minority group, numbering less than half of the U.S. population. Cultural contributions of people whose ancestors came from south of the United States will clearly contribute a strong flavor to the twenty-first-century American salad bowl.

It is hard to say what the specific role of South American immigrants will be in this new reality. Many South Americans today focus their sense of identity on their place of origin. They may think of themselves as *peruanos* (Peruvians) or Cabeños (immigrants from the Peruvian town of Cabanaconde). But South Americans in the United States find they are lumped into the larger categories of "Latinos" or "Hispanics" by their neighbors. The much larger immigrant populations from Mexico, Cuba, and Puerto Rico tend to dominate the Hispanic markets and media. It will be a challenge for South American immigrants to retain their sense of distinct South American identity.

It is also difficult to guess what the future pattern of emigration from South America will be. That will largely depend on whether South American nations can stabilize their governments and economies. The continuing political struggles of Ecuador and the har-

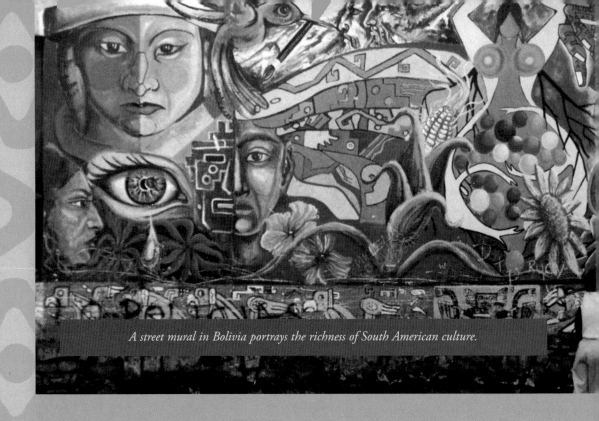

A street mural in Bolivia portrays the richness of South American culture.

rowing violence in Colombia offer little reason for optimism at this time. On the other hand, Brazil, Argentina, and Chile seem to be moving ahead toward the future as prosperous and stable democratic nations. If South American countries can rise above the troubles of their past and increase in prosperity, South Americans will have fewer reasons to uproot and relocate in the United States. Whatever future patterns of immigration turn out to be, however, the descendants of today's South American immigrants will increasingly enjoy the benefits and expand on the opportunities of life in the United States.

Habla Español

el futuro (ale foo-too-rah): the future

felicidad (fay-lee-see-dod): happiness

Timeline

1492–1820—Europeans capture and sell between 10 and 15 million Africans into slavery in the Americas.

November 1452—Francisco Pizarro and his men arrive at Cajamarca and slaughter the Inca.

1498—Christopher Columbus sails into Gulf of Paria, now part of Venezuela.

1544—Diego Hualpa discovers silver lode at Cerro Rico outside Potosí, Bolivia.

1615—The Dutch establish the first European colony in Guyana.

1819—Simón Bolívar leads first raid across the Andes to defeat the Spanish troops in Bogotá.

1904—Christ of the Andes monument is dedicated on the Argentine-Chilean border.

1970—Salvador Allende is elected president of Chile.

1972—President Richard Nixon uses the phrase "War on Drugs" for the first time.

September 1973—A coup overthrows the government of Salvador Allende in Chile.

1988—U.S.-backed opposition forces overthrows the government of Augusto Pinochet in Chile.

Further Reading

Cullison, Alan. *The South Americans*. New York: Chelsea House, 1991.

Figueredo, D. H. *The Complete Idiot's Guide to Latino History and Culture*. Indianapolis: Alpha Books, 2002.

Meyer, Nicholas E. *Biographical Dictionary of Hispanic Americans*. New York: Checkmark Books, 2001.

Nava, Yolanda. *It's All in the Frijoles: 100 Famous Latinos Share Real-Life Stories*. New York: Simon & Schuster, 2000.

Stavans, Ilan and Lalo Alcaraz, Illustrator. *Latino USA: A Cartoon History*. New York: Basic Books, 2000.

Wood, Michael. *Conquistadors*. Berkeley and Los Angeles: University of California Press, 2000.

For More Information

American Friends' Service Committee
www.afsc.org

BBC News—Americas Directory
news.bbc.co.uk/2/hi/americas

Center for Immigration Studies
www.cis.org

Hispanic Online
www.hispaniconline.com

Los Latinos USA: A Celebration of Latino Pride
www.spanishclassonline.com/usa.htm

National Network for Immigrant and Refugee Rights
www.nnirr.org

U.S. Census Bureau Public Information Office
www.census.gov

Video: *Transnational Fiesta: 1992*
University of California Extension
Center for Media and Independent Learning
2000 Center St., 4th Floor
Berkeley, CA 94704
(510) 642-0460

Publisher's note:
The Web sites listed on this page were active at the time of publication. The publisher is not responsible for Web sites that have changed their addresses or discontinued operation since the date of publication. The publisher will review the Web sites and update the list upon each reprint.

Index

Biographies

Kenneth and Marsha McIntosh are freelance writers living in Flagstaff, Arizona. Marsha lived in Lima, Peru, as a teenager. She has taught in the Migrant Workers Tutorial Program in Minneapolis, Minnesota, and was Assistant Coordinator for the CASS program, working with students from Central America and the Caribbean at Broome Community College in upstate New York. She has also served as interpreter for groups of Americans doing social justice projects in Guatemala, Honduras, and Peru. Kenneth taught English and ESL (English as a Second Language) for a decade in Los Angeles County, California, where most of his students were Latinos, many of them recent immigrants from Latin America. The McIntoshes have also served as a host family for students from Central America and will be traveling to Guatemala for the wedding of one of their "host daughters." They enjoy living in northern Arizona with its mix of Hispanic and American Indian cultures.

Dr. José E. Limón is professor of Mexican-American Studies at the University of Texas at Austin where he has taught for twenty-five years. He has authored over forty articles and three books on Latino cultural studies and history. He lectures widely to academic audiences, civic groups, and K–12 educators.

Picture Credits

Benjamin Stewart: pp. 16, 17, 18, 65, 66, 83, 84, 85, 87

Clipart.com: p. 37

Corbis: pp. 36, 47, 71, 74

Corel: pp. 9, 13, 22, 29, 31, 32, 40, 50, 59, 61, 77, 91, 103

Dianne Hodack: p. 6

Imageexpress.com: p. 63

Marsha McIntosh: pp. 56, 64, 72, 73, 88

PhotoDisc: p. 39

Photos.com: pp. 23, 27, 49, 52, 57, 58, 60

The Records of the Offices of the Government of Puerto Rico in the U.S., Centro de Estudios Puertorriqueños, Hunter College, CUNY, Photographer unknown: p. 25

Roxanna Stevens: p. 51

Viola Ruelke Gommer: p. 69